# Kingdom Kidz Bible

### with envelope surprises!

# Noah

## Genesis 6:9–9:17

PROMISE PRESS

An Imprint of Barbour Publishing

The world was filled with people who didn't love God.
They didn't obey God's laws. They didn't do good
things.

But Noah was different! Noah loved God with all his
heart. Noah obeyed God's laws and did good things.

One day God told Noah to build an ark. Noah obeyed God and did exactly what God said.

Bang, bang, bang! Pound, pound, pound! Saw, saw, saw! With his hammer and saw, Noah built the ark.

God told Noah to bring two of every animal inside the ark.

"Moo! Moo!" said the cows.

"Oink! Oink!" said the pigs.

"Hiss! Hiss!" said the snakes.

"R-O-A-R!" said the lions.

When Noah and the animals were tucked inside the ark, God shut the door.

Down, down, down splashed the rain, but the ark floated safely through the storm.

Finally, the rain stopped and God told Noah to bring all the animals out of the ark.

Noah obeyed God. He did exactly what God said because Noah loved God with all his heart.

The sun shone again. God painted a rainbow across the sky especially for Noah.

Noah obeyed God's laws, and I want to obey God's laws, too. Today I pray, **Dear God, I want to obey You because I love You with all my heart. Amen.**